The Gospel
and the Poor

The Gospel
and the Poor

Wolfgang Stegemann

**Translated by
Dietlinde Elliott**

FORTRESS PRESS   **PHILADELPHIA**

This book is a translation of *Das Evangelium und die Armen: Uber den Ursprung der Theologie der Armen im Neuen Testament* by Wolfgang Stegemann. Copyright © 1981 by Chr. Kaiser Verlag, Munich, West Germany.

English translation copyright © 1984 by Fortress Press

Library of Congress Cataloging in Publication Data

Stegemann, Wolfgang, 1945–
  The gospel and the poor.

  Translation of: Das Evangelium und die Armen.
  1. Poor—Biblical teaching.   2. Bible.   N.T.—Criticism, interpretation, etc.   I. Title.
BS2545.P65S7313   1984   261.8'34569   83–48915
ISBN 0–8006–1783–5

K457D84   Printed in the United States of America   1–1783

to
Willy Schottroff

Contents

8   CONTENTS

Preface

This book is the result of several talks I gave for various groups. An interest in the theology of the poor has prompted my hosts as well as me to ground our own positions in the Bible. In order to provide a brief overview of the whole New Testament tradition concerning a theology of the poor, it was necessary to present much of the material in the form of theses, so to speak. Some of the interpretations of New Testament texts may strike the reader as unfamiliar. The endnotes are limited to a few references and supporting evidence.

I dedicate this study to my friend Willy Schottroff on the occasion of his fiftieth birthday.

WOLFGANG STEGEMANN
June 1981, Heidelberg

Editorial Note

In this volume those people in the Gospels who have no perceived status in society (the sick, children, slaves, women, and so forth)—often unnamed—are referred to as "the little people" (*die kleinen Leute*); they are the "least" and the "lowest" by societal standards. The Greek term for them, as Stegemann points out, is *penētes*. For further insightful commentary on "the little people," see David Rhoads and Donald Michie, *Mark as Story* (Philadelphia: Fortress Press, 1982), 129–35.

In the endnotes (notes 23, 50, and 77) the editor has added several bibliographic entries not referred to in the original by the author. They represent recent and readily available English-language works relevant to the author's interests and concerns. These entries appear in brackets.

The designations "before the Common Era" (B.C.E.) and "Common Era" (C.E.) are used to indicate the shared history of Jews and Christians across the centuries. These are more inclusive and universal designations than B.C. and A.D.

The Poor
and the Gospel

Poverty—An Ambiguous Term

"Poverty" is an ambiguous term. In its original meaning it refers to the external, economic, and social circumstances in which people live. The real-life situation described by this term, however, depends on the specific socioeconomic condition of society as a whole and on the social status of the person using the term.

Thus, in late nineteenth-century Germany, for instance, an impoverished nobleman and a poor weaver had little in common. While the weaver found himself "down and out," barely surviving from day to day, the impoverished nobleman seemed to be rich from the weaver's perspective. Seen by his peers, however, the nobleman was considered poor since he could not maintain the life style appropriate to his social position. In both of these instances, the term "poor" indicates a place in society that is identifiable in material and social ways.

Beyond that, "poverty" may also be used in the figurative sense. This is usually indicated, however, by appropriate qualifiers, such as *"emotionally* impoverished," or it is evident from the immediate context. And in those cases where poverty or uncompromising frugality is viewed as the ideal way of life, be it for religious reasons (for example, mendicant friars) or for reasons of political philosophy (for example, Cynics), a corresponding material situation must always be presumed: a relation to societal life is also always present, implicitly or explicitly.

New Testament Terms for "Poor"

The Greek term most commonly used in the New Testament for "poor" is *ptōchos*. The term used most often in the literature of ancient Greece *(penēs)* occurs only in 2 Cor. 9:9, in a quotation from the Old Testament. A related term, *penichros*, also occurs only once in the New Testament (Luke 21:2). The term for "poor" *(apōros)* preferred by the Jewish historian Flavius Josephus is not used anywhere in the New Testament. In Acts 4:34, in reference to the "community of goods," we come across an expression for "needy" *(endeēs)*.

This range of terms used in the New Testament is illuminating for several reasons. The predominant use of *ptōchos* in the New Testament for "poverty" has its basis, as I will show, in the real-life situation of the people under discussion: they are desperately poor, wretched creatures who are fighting for their survival. The ancient Greek term *(penēs)* would have been quite inadequate to describe such circumstances, since Greek literature, for the most part, distinguishes between the destitute *(ptōchos)*, one who has nothing, and one who has little and must live frugally *(penēs)*. The latter folk *(penētes)* included small farmers and artisans who depended upon their own labor and as a rule had to eke out a living. Their counterparts were the rich *(plousioi)* who lived from their wealth and were able to employ others in support of their own easy life.

The extreme antithesis of these rich were the destitute *(ptōchoi)*.[1] They are known to have existed already in classical antiquity, but it seems that the number of these destitute folk had increased considerably by the Roman imperial period.

Therefore, the predominant use of *ptōchos* in the New Testament has to be understood also as a reflection of a social reality.[2]

Poor in the Metaphorical Sense

In most cases the terms for "poor" in the New Testament are used in their original, socioeconomic sense. One exception occurs in Gal. 4:9, where Paul labels the "elemental spirits" *(stoicheia)* as "beggarly" *(ptōcha)*. On the other hand, I am not convinced that Paul's remark on the poverty of Jesus (2 Cor. 8:9) is intended to be taken only metaphorically. The controversy concerning the beatitude of the "poor in spirit" *(oi ptōchoi tō pneumati)* in Matt. 5:3 is well known. Obviously, it does not refer to material poverty. Yet it would be a mistake to use this particular passage as the basis for a "spiritualized" interpretation of the other passages on poverty in the Gospels. Furthermore, it should be noted that just this metaphorical use of poverty terminology in the New Testament reveals links between the ancient reader and the actual situation of the poor. Thus, the label "beggarly" for the "elemental spirits" in Gal. 4:9 is related to a term for "powerless," "weak," and "sick" *(asthenēs)*. In 2 Cor. 8:9 a contrast is presupposed between destitute *(ptōchos)* and rich *(plousios)*. This is typical for the entire New Testament as well as other ancient texts. That same opposition is argued in Rev. 3:17. Here, too, the rich man who has no need is contrasted to the poor man. In Rev. 3:17, particularly, the circumstances of the destitute are vividly portrayed. The term *ptōchos* is used in the same breath with others that collectively refer to the plight of the poor: one who is wretched *(ho talaipōros)*, pitiable *(ho eleeinos)*, blind *(typhlos)*, and naked *(gymnos)*. This characterization—even though in this instance it may be used metaphorically—is an extremely realistic description of poverty as it was taken for granted throughout the New Testament. The poor person is wretched and miserable, sick and poorly clothed. And, we may add, he or she lacks life's most basic necessities, being a beggar and totally dependent on alms.

The Poor Are Sick

Elsewhere in the New Testament, too, the poor are mentioned in one breath with the sick; the maimed, the blind, the lame, and others—all are numbered with the poor (Luke 14:13, 21; 4:18–19; 7:22; Matt. 11:5; 25:35; see also Gal. 4:9). Luke 14:12–13 contains the exhortation to invite precisely this "gallery" of the poor to the banquet, rather than friends, relatives, and rich neighbors. And Luke 14:21–23 implies that, apart from *the local poor*—the crippled, the blind, and the lame—there were also the *itinerant* poor: "Go out to the highways and hedges, and compel people to come in" (v. 23).[3]

Lazarus, this personification of a poor man, lies ill at the door of a rich man and waits to eat from the latter's scraps (Luke 16:20). Therefore, overly subtle differentiation between those destitute who are not yet sick on the one hand, and the blind, the lame, and the crippled on the other, is hardly meaningful. Conversely, it is likely that in many New Testament passages that treat of the poor, particularly in the Gospels, precisely this social milieu of the destitute is implied. Many of Jesus' healings occur in this setting (Luke 4:31–37, 38–42; 5:12–16, 17–26; 6:6–11, 18–19). The account of the blind beggar Bartimaeus is an especially vivid portrayal of this correlation (Mark 10:46–52; see also Matt. 20:29–34 [9:27–31] and Luke 18:35–43). Without doubt, antiquity had known of the practice of maiming infants (mostly abandoned ones) and of their subsequent exploitation as beggars. The elder Seneca describes this procedure in all its gruesome detail in his *Controversies* (10:4). Yet nowhere in the New Testament do we encounter a rancor toward these sick beggars that is comparable to Seneca's remarks.

The Poor Are Naked

The plight of the destitute person is aptly portrayed in Rev. 3:17 when it states that he or she is naked *(gymnos)*. To be sure, the blind Bartimaeus still had his coat *(himation,* Mark 10:50). In a Palestinian context this seems to distinguish him from the majority, however, since such an outer garment was all but unattainable by a beggar. In fact, Luke 3:11 no longer reckons with such a precious possession when John the Baptist exhorts the crowd: "He who has two coats *(chitōn),* let him share with him who has none; and he who has food, let him do likewise." To be "naked"—undoubtedly to be clothed only in rags, left to freeze in the cold (James 2:16)—is the mark of the poor. This is also clear from James 2:15 and Matt. 25:36. Job (24:10) already assumes that the poor person literally loses the last shirt—right off his or her back—to the creditors (see also Matt. 5:40). In Matt. 6:25 (see also Luke 12:22) it is also assumed that the poor who are addressed have nothing to wear:

> Therefore I tell you, do not be anxious about your life, what you shall eat or what you shall drink, nor about your body, what you shall put on. Is not life more than food, and the body more than clothing?

The Poor Are Hungry

Often in the New Testament an immediate connection is made between the lack of clothing and an utter lack of sustenance. Poverty is synonymous with being *hungry* (and thirsty). This association is made in Luke 3:11. We come upon it again in Matt. 6:25 and 25:35–36 and in James 2:15–16. The beatitude concerning the poor in Luke 6:20—"Blessed are you poor, for yours is the kingdom of God"—characterizes the circumstances of the poor; they are in sorrow and want of food. The poor do not know from one day to the next whether they will eat or drink; they are always on the verge of starvation (Matt. 6:25–26). This is the situation of the poor when James 2:15–16 describes them as naked and without daily sustenance, lacking the essentials for physical survival ("ill clad and in lack of daily food").

The Poor Are Destitute

To be poverty-stricken *(ptōchos)*, in New Testament terms, is to be destitute. Such people depended on alms for even the basics of life. For this, too, there are vivid examples: apart from those beggars already mentioned, Bartimaeus and Lazarus, there is the lame beggar in the Temple in Jerusalem whom Peter heals in the name of Jesus (Acts 3:1–10). Alms might be given (and received) in the form of food and clothes as well as money (only Mark 14:7; see also Matt. 25:35–36; Luke 16:20; and Acts 3:1–10).

Thus, the face of poverty as presented in the New Testament is basically this: the poor are destitute, always close to starvation, often identified along with the disabled and the severely ill, poorly clothed, and dependent on the help of strangers.

Our comprehensive information concerning the circumstances of the destitute in antiquity that is communicated by the Synoptic Gospels, and comes through no other documents of this time, has nothing at all to do with the fact that this group of wretched people made up a notable portion of the society at that time. On the contrary, we seek in vain for an equally apparent special *interest* in the poor in other contemporary texts—outside of Judaism that is. The special significance of the poor for the good news (gospel) of Jesus Christ must be understood against the background of the socioeco-

nomic and religious (Jewish) origins of the Christian movement. This becomes particularly clear in the special way in
which this movement historically originated within Palestinian
Judaism, and, more specifically, within Galilee. Yet it also
contains significance for the self-understanding of later Christian communities beyond Palestine. To state the case somewhat
provocatively: the Jesus movement in this particular form—that
of a religious movement of the poor—could only have originated within Palestinian Judaism at the beginning of the Common Era.

It is impossible here to investigate in depth the economic
and political causes of the pauperization of large segments of
the Palestinian population at the beginning of the Common
Era.[4] The following factors, I believe, were of supreme significance:

1. The radical reorganization of Palestine introduced by
Pompey (he subdued Judea in 63 B.C.E.) deprived the Jewish
state of the coastal cities and the Dekapolis. This severely
curtailed trade and resulted in a great number of dispossessed
farmers (see Schalit and Applebaum).

2. Herod the Great's expropriation of enormous stretches of
farmland which were then sold to wealthy landowners (Josephus, *Antiquities* XVII.307,355; XVIII.2) led to huge con-
centrations of land in the hands of a few (see Theissen).
This in turn created great numbers of dependent tenant farmers (see Kippenberg).

3. The crushing burden of taxes, whether imposed by the
Herodian dynasty or by the Romans themselves, is of considerable significance. It was instrumental in causing re-
sistance among the impoverished peasants and tenant farmers
against the foreign Roman rule and its domestic collaborators
(see Kreissig, Theissen, Kippenberg, Hengel, and others).

4. Crop failures all but ruined the small farmers and tenants,

and the artisans who depended on them in the rural areas
(ecological crises according to Theissen and Jeremias).

In principle, the causes for the pauperization of large segments of the Palestinian population hardly vary from those
outside of Palestine. John Chrysostom (344–407 C.E.) in his
commentary on Matthew offers a vivid description of the circumstances of these people in his own time, one which no
doubt applies to several preceding centuries as well:

> But will ye that we leave these too, and go to others who seem
> to be more just? Who then are they? They that are possessed of
> lands, and reap the wealth that springs from the earth. And what
> can be more unjust than these? For if any one were to examine
> how they treat their wretched and toilworn laborers, he will see
> them to be more cruel than savages. For upon them that are
> pining with hunger, and toiling throughout all their life, they
> both impose constant and intolerable payments, and lay on them
> laborious burdens, and like asses or mules, or rather like stones,
> do they treat their bodies, allowing them not so much as to draw
> breath a little, and when the earth yields, and when it doth not
> yield, they alike wear them out, and grant them no indulgence.
> And what can be more pitiable than this, when after having
> labored throughout the whole winter, and being consumed with
> frost and rain, and watchings, they go away with their hands
> empty, yea moreover in debt, and fearing and dreading more
> than this famine and shipwreck, the torments of the overlookers,
> and their dragging them about, and their demands, and their
> imprisonments, and the services from which no entreaty can
> deliver them!
> Why should one speak of the merchandise which they make
> of them, the sordid gains which they gain by them, by their
> labors and their sweat filling winepresses, and wine vats, but not
> suffering them to take home so much as a small measure, but
> draining off the entire fruits into the casks of their wickedness,
> and flinging to them for this a little money?
> And new kinds of usuries also do they devise, and not lawful
> even according to the laws of the heathens, and they frame
> contracts for loans full of many a curse. For not the hundredth
> part of the sum, but the half of the sum they press for and exact;

and this when he of whom it is exacted has a wife, if bringing up children, is a human being, and is filling their threshing floor, and their winepress by his own toils.

But none of these things do they consider. Wherefore now it were seasonable to bring forward the prophet and say, "Be astonished, 0 Heaven, and be horribly afraid, 0 earth," to what great brutality hath the race of man been madly carried away![5]

Good News
for the Poor

Theological Confrontation with Poverty
in the New Testament

In the New Testament two basic possibilities of theological confrontation with poverty are discernible:

1. The gospel is the basis and expression of the hope, self-consciousness, and solidarity among the poor themselves.

2. The gospel is the basis and expression of awareness of the circumstances of the poor and of solidarity with them.

Each possibility presupposes a different social situation of its "representative groups." A literary determination of these groups can be made with reference to time and place and with regard to their historical documentation in the New Testament.

1. The "representatives" of the "gospel of the poor" are themselves poor (*ptōchoi*). They are the first- and second-generation followers of Jesus in Palestine. We know about them via the allegedly oldest tradition of Jesus of Nazareth, which is preserved in the Synoptic Gospels, as well as via the "Sayings Source" ("L" Source = common to both Matthew and Luke apart from Mark). The time frame of these followers of Jesus may be fixed in approximately the second third of the first century of the Common Era (and prior to the Jewish-

Roman War culminating in the destruction of Jerusalem in 70
C.E.).

2. Apart from a few wealthy persons, the "representatives"
of the gospel are Christian groups outside Palestine who are
not *ptōchoi* but predominantly *penētes* (2 Cor. 9:9). Rudi-
ments of this gospel are evident in the Pauline letters, but it
is most prominent later in the Gospels according to Matthew
and Luke (see also the Letter of James). The time frame for
these groups is probably between 50 and 100 C.E.

Poverty and the Jesus Movement in Palestine

The Messianic Movement of the Poor

The movement within Judaism in Palestine associated with
the name of Jesus was a movement *of the poor for the poor*.
Apart from the son of a certain carpenter from Nazareth (Mark
6:3), its figureheads are some fishermen from Galilee (Mark
1:16–20), a minor customs employee (Mark 2:13–14), and a
zealot (Mark 3:18). Women, too, belonged from the very beginning (Mark 15:40–41).

The fact that Jesus, as the son of a carpenter, was probably
a carpenter is often used as evidence that he himself was not
among the poor. Thus, his solidarity with them was supposedly
of "ethical" and "partisan" origin. And, indeed, an important
proof for this position is the indisputable fact that the occu-
pation of carpenter was not a despised one. It proves nothing,
however, about the material circumstances of a carpenter. It
is therefore with good reason that the following has been noted:

> Thus, Jesus is an artisan, not very privileged, but by the same
> token not one of the despised. Yet it must be noted that Nazareth
> must have been an insignificant Galilean hamlet. . . . The social
> circumstances of a carpenter in such a place must be assessed
> accordingly.[6]

In principle, one has to assess the economic well-being of any craft by the degree to which it is utilized, or can be utilized, given the material circumstances of its patrons. This is especially true if (with Kippenberg[7]) we assume that in the villages of Palestine the labor of an artisan was repaid with a share of the harvest. Thus, the social circumstances of the village clan determined that of the artisans within it. Generally speaking, given what we know about the social circumstances of the Palestinian peasantry of this time, severe poverty rather than material comfort is implied here.

The occupational designation *tektōn* may refer to either a "carpenter" within the building profession or to a "cabinet-maker." In both cases we may infer the situation of a *wage-earning day laborer*, unless one wants to postulate the above-named clan-situation for so late a date.[8]

Probably neither Jesus nor his first disciples were professional beggars, yet they shared the desperate situation of many of their fellow country folk—particularly in Galilee—barely avoiding utter poverty. This plight of the Jesus people is highlighted, for instance, in the conflict over the Sabbath in Mark 2:23–28 (see note 11). It may also be the background for the cursing of the fig tree in Mark 11:12–14. The hunger of Jesus and his disciples is not an accident—say, because they had forgotten to buy provisions for the Sabbath, or because Jesus had neglected to eat breakfast in Bethany. This is the hunger and plight of the poor. One should also note the church historian Eusebius's quotation of Hegesippus, which speaks of the poor relatives of Jesus:

> Now there still survived of the family of the Lord grandsons of Judas, who was said to have been his brother according to the flesh, and they were delated [that is, informed against] as being of the family of David. These the officer [= *evocatus*] brought to Domitian Caesar, for, like Herod, he was afraid of the coming of the Christ. He asked them if they were of the house of David and they admitted it. . . . They then showed him their hands,

adducing as testimony of their labour the hardness of their bodies, and the tough skin which had been embossed on their hands from their incessant work. . . . At this Domitian did not condemn them at all, but despised them as simple folk, released them, and decreed an end to the persecution against the church.[9]

Incidentally, John Chrysostom also regarded Jesus and his disciples as "unknown people from poor families."[10] Initially, the Jesus movement was active locally near its immediate place of origin on the shores of Lake Galilee. Its addressees were largely identical with its sympathizers: the popular masses who took no offense, for instance, at the association of the Jesus people with tax collectors and sinners. Their disputes with other Jewish reform movements, especially the Pharisaic movement, did not center on the validity of the Law (Torah) as such, but on the needs of the moment. This becomes especially clear in the disputes about the Sabbath which have been reported from the point of view of the Jesus movement (see, for example, Mark 2:23–28). The plight of the poor became the principle of interpretation of the Law (Torah) as God's gracious instruction for living.[11]

Yet this required more than the normative power of facts: it required the messianic self-consciousness of the poor, who discovered themselves as the objects of God's saving will. The expedition of the Jesus people toward Jerusalem, therefore, did not represent an advance into the center of power by a group of vainglorious and militant revolutionists. Rather, in Jerusalem they expected the epiphany of the God of Israel in his city. In the name of God their prophet-protagonist entered Jerusalem in messianic triumph as the pretender to the throne of David (Mark 11:7–10). In this respect the advance is comparable, for instance, to that of poor Jews from Cyrene who went into the wilderness under the leadership of Jonathan the Weaver and waited there for signs and wonders.[12]

Indeed, even the *demise* of Jesus points to this lofty claim of the movement, even though the movement made no attempt to force its success. From the point of view of the Romans, success was quite immaterial in any case, as was demonstrated also by the carnage wrought among the adherents of Jonathan. The crucifixion of Jesus as "King of the Jews" was neither a miscarriage of justice nor a cynical act of those in power: fear of the destabilization of the exploitative alliance of colonial rulers and wealthy domestic collaborators demanded law and order in the land.[13]

The Hope of the Poor

Just as John the Baptist had clashed with Herod, so Jesus had entered into a fatal conflict with the Roman backers of Herod's dynasty. The popularity of both Jesus and John with the masses had to do with the fact that they expected a change of regime from the point of view of "the little people." The expected liberation was not envisioned as strictly nationalistic, where only the masters change but the lot of the slaves remains the same. The messianic thrust of the Jesus movement was aimed primarily at a radical social transformation within Israel:

> He has put down the mighty from
>   their thrones,
> and exalted those of low degree;
> he has filled the hungry with good
>   things,
> and the rich he has sent empty away.
>   (Luke 1:52–53)[14]

Even after the crucifixion of Jesus, this socially revolutionary messianism remained intact, and its symbolic personification, Jesus of Nazareth, remained alive in the hearts of his followers. The prophetic proclaimer became the prophet proclaimed—who would soon return as divine judge in the clouds of heaven. A criticism that views this merely as the "projection" of unfulfilled worldly expectations into a heavenly or fantastic other world is actually not critical enough. It separates the hope of the poor from its object; for the poor of Palestine the first object was to learn even to hope.

Note that even the blind beggar Bartimaeus (Mark 10:46) began to scream when he heard "Jesus of Nazareth is here." The story about Bartimaeus is told from Bartimaeus's point of view for those who share his miserable experience—and now also his hope. Bartimaeus, the one who hopes, is the center of this story, and his hope is concrete insofar as its focal point is Jesus as the Son of David. The story's interest is in Bartimaeus's own fate and its transformation; he wants to see again, and his faith finally accomplishes that for him. The story does not relate an isolated medical miracle. It does not tell of the miracle-working powers of Jesus (as does Mark 8:22–26), but gives an account of the *wondrous transformation of the lot* of a blind beggar. In this sense the story is an expression of the hope of poor Jews in Palestine; in itself it embodies hope. In the healing of the blind man the eagerly anticipated coming of the kingdom of God had already become visible for those who told it to each other. "The blind receive their sight and the lame walk, . . . and the poor have good news [the gospel] preached to them" (Matt. 11:5 and Luke 4:18–19).

This is not wishful thinking conjured up out of the Hebrew Bible. Instead, the poor interpret their experience with the help of their religious tradition, understanding it as being open to the future, rather than the "beyond." Their experience included a solidarity which meant sharing the last morsel in the face of common want (Luke 3:11). On this basis the miracle of the multiplication of loaves was made possible, in which many were filled from a few loaves (Mark 6:34–44). Along with the healings of the most wretched, this solidarity among the poor themselves and with the despised prompted great expectations; and these expectations focused on the imminent "reign of God" *(basileia tou theou)*, in which those now hungry will laugh and be satisfied (Luke 6:20), and the poor will find compensation for their misery: then the last shall be first (Matt. 20:16).

The Self-Consciousness of the Poor

In many respects our portrait of the earliest Jesus movement necessarily remains obscure. Its organization derived from Israel becomes more tangible; its faith and life may be reconstructed from the "Sayings Source." Even more so than that of the earliest Jesus movement, which was still struggling for its own sense of hope, the convictions of the prophetic charismatics were shaped by a mood of crisis. This sense of crisis resulted from experiences of estrangement as well as from the increasing crisis situation in all of Jewish society after the destruction of Jerusalem in 70 C.E. In the face of a depressing and paralyzing present in which hunger and violence dominated their everyday experience, "the little people" held fast to their hope in the efficacious goodness of God. They castigated the rich and their "service of mammon" which amounted to idolatry, since thereby they worshiped another Lord than the Father in heaven. The thought and life of these charismatic prophets were based on their trust in the one Lord, the God of Israel, in the face of whose power even hunger and the fear of death lost their meaning. Their uncompromising attitude toward the rich was not envy, nor was their powerful expectation of "the last judgment" an expression of fantasies of revenge with a religious twist. They lived like "sheep among wolves," yet they never ceased to call all Israel to "repentance."

The sublime religious claim of these charismatics, exemplified particularly in their proclamation of judgment against Israel, corresponded to the *self-consciousness* of these poor. They were the messengers of the coming royal rule of God, proclaiming the message of peace in the hovels of Palestine—a message authenticated by their own life style. Their addressees were, as in the case of the earliest Jesus movement, primarily the impoverished masses. While they could offer them no bread and butter, they did offer the principle that human beings do not live by bread alone, that the care for daily bread, as well as the "service of mammon," must not become an all-consuming preoccupation (Matt. 6:25–34 and Luke 12:22–31). This message, too, was authenticated in the name of Jesus through the existence of the itinerant prophets. Indeed, they did without the "provisions" which even a beggar would attempt: barefoot and without a bag or a staff for protection against wild animals, they lived with a radical trust in the God of Israel, *their* heavenly Father. To the poor they gave back the human dignity of which they had been stripped through hunger and want.

The Significance of Jesus for the Poor

So far my sketch of discipleship in Palestine purposely does not characterize this movement of the poor as "christocentric," that is, concentrating on the particular significance of Jesus the Christ. Obviously, this is not to deny the special position of Jesus. He was doubtless the prophetic and messianic initiator of this movement and was seen by his followers as the eschatological King of Israel. As such he is named "Son of David" and "Son of God." This context also explains his title of "Messiah" (= "Christ"). These "titles" stress Jesus' commission in God's royal reign over Israel as legitimized by the God of Israel. Thus, the title "Son of Man" emphasizes his function as judge in the apocalyptic drama which was forecast by the prophets of the "Sayings Source" and fulfilled in gruesomely profane fashion in the Jewish-Roman War by the armies of the Roman oppressors (64–74 C.E.) By his preaching and practice of healing, Jesus of Nazareth gave motive and substance to the hopes focused on him. Thus, he was not merely the "symbol" of corresponding projections on the part of his followers. For them he was the prophetic Messiah; in him the hopes of the poor were soon to become reality; in his person the claim to God's kingdom which they awaited was a living reality—the messianic kingdom of the poor.

A few historical comments only are in order here. The historian cannot make pronouncements about the "eternal" truth of this claim, not even about its significance for the present, but must draw conclusions from the hopes, convictions, and faith of the ancient followers of Jesus. In so doing, the historian finds that the "messianic" claim of Jesus and his followers was primarily *socially* oriented, that it aimed for the reversal of the contemporary social order with a focus on eradicating the misery of the poor. In other words, the historian sees here the hope of poor Jews still developing and finds that they learned precisely this hope as a result of the preaching and practice of Jesus—words and deeds.

Even after the death of Jesus this situation remains basically unchanged. For the itinerant prophets of the "Sayings Source," too, the basis of their message to Israel continued to be Jesus of Nazareth. And for them he also became the one who is to come (Luke 13:34–45 and Matt. 23:37–39), the coming Son of Man (Luke 11:29–32 and Matt. 12:38–42). Yet their justifiable expectations concerning the judgment day of the Son of Man did not bring to mind a doomsday and did not point to an otherworldly kingdom. Rather, they reckoned with the *historical* coming of the Son of Man and anticipated the reign of God on earth. For this they struggled with their whole being, sometimes at the risk of their lives. Indeed, they did not do this with a view to the compensation of their present misery after death; much less did they feed their fellow sufferers in Israel with such hopes. Nor did they expect the coming of some "mythological" figure: they already knew who this Son of

Man was—Jesus of Nazareth who had to perish in Jerusalem like every other prophet. For this hope they perceived reason and substance in the preaching, ministry, and destiny of Jesus of Nazareth. In this respect he continued to be present in their stories of him and their hope in him, not in an abstract creed but in a living conviction and its convicting life.

Poverty and Christian Discipleship in the Roman Empire

A New Consensus on the Social Status of Early Christians

A new consensus seems to be developing in the assessment of the social provenance of the first Christians outside of Palestine. According to this consensus, the Christian groups were definitely made up of all the social strata of contemporary urban society, but they were upwardly mobile. For example, Wilhelm Wuellner conjectures that the Corinthian Christians came "by and large from fairly well-to-do bourgeois circles, with a fair percentage also from upper-class people, as well as the very poor." He also rejects the use of 1 Cor. 1:26 ("not many of you were wise . . . not many were powerful, not many were of noble birth") as a proof text for "the proposition of Christianity's low proletarian origins."[15]

E. A. Judge, a professor of ancient history, does not believe that Paul is talking here about "actual facts." Instead, he considers this formulation to be rhetorical (in my opinion correctly so). Yet he seems to consider 1 Cor. 1:27–28 ("God chose what is foolish in the world, . . . what is weak . . . what is low and despised . . . ") to be rhetorical as well. In his opinion the Corinthians neither considered themselves, nor were considered by their contemporaries, as "unintelligent nonentities.'' Thus, he reaches the following conclusion about the Christians of that time:

> Far from being a socially depressed group, then, if the Corinthians are at all typical, the Christians were dominated by a socially pretentious section of the population of the big cities. Beyond that they seem to have drawn on a broad constituency, probably representing the household dependents of the leading members.[16]

Judge correctly points out that these dependents and slaves ''were by no means the most debased section of society.'' To the contrary, the slaves as members of the urban household *(oikos)* enjoyed a certain measure of material security compared to the most underprivileged class, the peasantry, which was made up of tenant farmers, persons in slavery on the land, and day laborers. These persons were largely untouched by Christianity at that time.[17] Theissen comes to similar conclusions, though in many respects he is more specific.[18] Kreissig sees the comfortably well-off urban ''middle class'' (artisans and merchants), rather than the ''proletariat,'' as the basic element of the Christian communities and believes that they included a considerable portion of the upper classes.[19]

The Early Christians in the Roman Empire Are ''The Little People''

Without a doubt, a closer look at the social composition of the early Christian communities is in order. In some areas it will be necessary to dig a little deeper. My tentative *thesis* is as follows: most of the early Christian communities were made up predominantly of ''the little people'' *(penētes)*, including neither the destitute *(ptōchoi)* nor the wealthy *(plousioi)*, with the exception of that branch of Christianity described by Luke. Moreover, it is only in Luke that we might even consider the presence of aristocratic *(euschēmōn)* and perhaps noble-born *(eugenēs)* Christians. A brief explanation of this thesis follows.

There Are No Destitute Among
the Early Christians

Neither in the Pauline congregations nor in those Christian communities that form the background of the Synoptic Gospels, nor even among the addressees of the Letter of James, can we expect to find the destitute *(ptōchoi)* reckoned as Christian contemporaries. Paul knows only a handful of such destitute folk *(ptōchoi)* among the "saints" in Jerusalem, for whom his congregations are arranging a collection (Rom. 15:25–29; 1 Cor. 16:1–4; 2 Cor. 8:1–15; 9:1–5; Gal. 2:10). When in 2 Cor. 8:2 Paul speaks of the "extreme poverty" *(hē kata bathous ptōcheia)* of the congregations in Macedonia, we must not therefore conclude that these communities consisted of beggars. After all, they did participate in the collection for Jerusalem. On the other hand, this phrase of Paul must not be interpreted as merely rhetorical exaggeration: one must assume that they were indeed very poor, though not to the point of destitution.

Nor are the Christian addressees of the Letter of James destitute. The destitute person *(ptōchos)* referred to in James 2:2, who might enter the assembly *(synagōgē)*, is an "outsider" (perhaps the passage is a reference to an actual incident).[20] If the Christians addressed in James were themselves destitute, it is not likely that the author would chide them for treating beggars with contempt (2:6). Moreover, there would be no need in this context to remind the readers that God has chosen "those who are poor in the world to be rich in faith and heirs of the kingdom" (2:5). And yet, does not James state expressly that he is concerned here with *Christian poor* (in 2:15, he speaks of brother and sister)? Even so, in view of 2:2, 5, it is not likely that the Christian destitute mentioned in 2:15 belonged to the Christian community of James; the characterization of these persons suggests that they *are* destitute *(ptōchoi)*. James argues a hypothetical case: if a brother or sister were naked and were lacking daily sustenance, you would hardly offer them pious platitudes instead of basic necessities (2:15–17). Assured of the consent of the readers to this hypothetical example, he then draws this conclusion: faith without works is impossible.[21]

Similarly, there are no destitute *(ptōchoi)* in those communities of Christians addressed by the authors of the Synoptic Gospels. In the Gospel of Luke, for instance, the beatitude of the destitute *(ptōchoi)* expressly refers to the disciples of Jesus, who, according to Luke, are voluntarily poor (6:20–31). With Luke we generally find that the destitute are beneficiaries of Christian charity but not themselves Christians, as is evident from 14:13–14 and 14:21–23.[22] The case is similar for Mark and Matthew. The poor whom the disciples will always have with them (Mark 14:7 and Matt. 26:11; see Deut. 15:11) are not disciples, representatives of contemporary Christianity, but are distinct from them and viewed as recipients of the disciples' alms. Matthew, too, no longer relates the beatitude of the poor—those who hunger and thirst—to the life situation of beggars, to which it originally referred (Matt. 5:3, 6).

There Are Also No Wealthy Christians (Except in Luke)

On the other hand, again with the exception of Luke,[23] we cannot presume the presence of *wealthy* members of the Christian communities outside of Palestine. The gulf between the Christians and the rich is made very explicit in the Letter of James: "Is it not the rich who oppress you [*katadynasteuein*],[24] is it not they who drag you into court?" (2:16). The rich also blaspheme the honorable name (of Christ) by which Christians are called (2:7). Furthermore, the wealthy who are addressed in James 5:1–6 are not Christians, as may be inferred from 2:7 as well as from 1:9–11, where the rich man is not called "brother." If James 4:13–17 is indeed referring to Christians (because of v. 15), then they are by no means rich. They are explicitly differentiated from the wealthy; see the identical beginnings of 4:13 and 5:1. Evidently, the reference here is to small merchants who did not differ from minor artisans—even in the port city of Alexandria, one of the metropolitan centers of that time.[25]

But what about 1 Cor. 1:26–29? Here Paul points out to the Corinthians their own social situation:

> For consider your call, brethren; not many of you were wise according to worldly standards, not many were powerful, not many were of noble birth; but God chose what is foolish in the world to shame the wise, God chose what is weak in the world to shame the strong, God chose what is low and despised in the world, even things that are not, to bring to nothing things that are so that no human being might boast in the presence of God.

The gist of this Pauline formulation, according to most scholars, is that among the Corinthian Christians there were "not many" *(ou polloi),* yet nevertheless some who were "wise" *(sophoi),* "powerful" *(dynatoi)*, and "of noble birth" *(eugeneis).*[26] In my opinion, however, precisely the use of the term "noble born" (Greek *eugenēs* = Latin *nobilis*) in this context calls for an ironic understanding of 1 Cor. 1:26. In contrast to Acts 17:11, it is used here not in the metaphorical sense—of noble conduct—but in the original sense—of noble origin of persons. In Luke 9:12 the term denotes someone like a prince who is looking to gain a kingdom in a foreign country. The high priests, for instance, are counted among the nobles by Josephus.[27] Erastus, the city treasurer from Corinth *(oikonomos tēs poleōs*, Rom. 16:23) is often cited as an example of a Christian noble in Corinth. This line of argumentation, however, is open to question: even the highest-ranking fiscal officers of the emperor were not nobles but predominantly freed slaves.[28] Theissen thinks this Erastus is identical with an aedile of Corinth by the same name who is identified by an inscription.[29] He considers him not a noble but rather from among the *dynatoi,* that is, the economically and socially powerful residents.[30] Even this classification of Erastus is not certain as Theissen himself points out. Consequently, even Erastus might have been a municipal slave or freedman. Ultimately, Paul's use of the term "noble born" *(eugenēs)* in 1 Cor. 1:26 remains the best indication that he is here reminding the Corinthians, with rhetorical irony, that without exception they belong to "the little people," and that among them there can be no reference to any who are wise, powerful, or noble—not even a few.

If there had really been *some* nobles or powerful persons among the Christians at Corinth, Paul's line of argumentation would have been rather odd in this context, to say the least. In this case he would be exposing these Christian brothers by counting them among those who are humbled by the election of the foolish, the weak, and the lowly born. Not even those social tensions in Corinth that are occasioned by the Lord's Supper, as seen in 1 Cor. 11:17, point to the existence of wealthy persons in this community. These tensions are easily explained from the social composition of a community that included slave and free as well as from the considerable social stratification within the groups of "the little people" *(penētes).* Even Stephanas, whose entire *house* was baptized by Paul (1 Cor. 1:15), was not necessarily a wealthy citizen, notwithstanding the fact that he might have seemed better off in the eyes of some of the other Christians in Corinth. From the perspective of the Christians in Macedonia, the Corinthians were better off than the Macedonians themselves. The Christians in Corinth, however, were not so well-off that they were spared worry about their own economic situation because of their gifts to the people in Jerusalem (2 Cor. 8:13). It is with good reason, therefore, that Paul characterizes the Corinthians as "the weak" which God has chosen. For by this phrase are meant "the little people" *(penētes)*,[31] in contrast to the "powerful" *(dynatoi)*, who are perceived to be economically and socially powerful and who certainly must be portrayed as wealthy.[32] Thus, a social gradation within the Corinthian community is only to be understood in terms of slaves, day laborers, clients, artisans, and small merchants.

Nor were there wealthy among the Christian groups from which we have received the Gospels of Matthew and Mark. The point of the story of "the rich youth" even in Mark (10:17–31) is no longer the problem of a rich person's discipleship, as it was originally (see also Matt. 19:16–30 and Luke 18:18–30). Thus, no rich person in the Markan community was obligated to identify with this story simply because there were no rich. (In this context see also Mark 4:18: it is the *Word* which bore no fruit in the wealthy, not "wealthy Christians who remained without fruit," that is, without "good works.") Accordingly, Mark is interested in the fate of the rich man only as an example. One who would attain "eternal life" fails because of his possessions; he, like all the rich, will not enter into the kingdom of God. Not so with the Christians of the Markan community. Their anxious question, "Then who can be saved?" prompted by the lot of the rich man, receives a positive answer: with God, even the impossible is possible (10:27). The subsequent context reveals that Mark is concerned here not with the rich but with the Christian addressees, for it is their particular situation that is discussed. They have left everything, have renounced their natural families (house and economic community) for the sake of their affiliation with the Christian community, and, moreover, they perceive themselves as persecuted (10:28–30). The words of Jesus in Mark point out to them that already now, in this present time, they regain what they have lost socially—indeed, even under persecution.

This is a reference to the community itself as the "family of God" (3:31–35). Accordingly, the community may also be assured of "eternal life" which the rich man will not attain. They, the "last," will be "first" (10:28–31).[33] It is not that Mark trivializes the problem of wealth; Mark and fellow Christians did not have the problem. Theirs was the problem of Christians who had experienced the pressures resulting from the chaos of the Jewish-Roman War, and who were prompted by this experience to ask questions about the end (of this eon) and about their own salvation.[34] By the same token the problem in Matt. 19:16–30 is no longer wealth. In Matthew the rich man turns out to be a shallow youth.[35]

People of Wealth and High Social Status
in the Lukan Community

In Luke's community alone, among the Christian communities, there might have been wealthy persons. Nowhere else in the New Testament is the life of the rich referred to and criticized in such detail. And since the great interest of Luke in criticizing the rich has as its objective their repentance (*metanoia;* see 16:19–31, esp. v. 30; as a paradigm: 19:1–10, the rich chief tax collector Zacchaeus), it is all the more likely that we are here dealing with a Christian audience. Finally, this is borne out in Luke 8:14. The addressees here referred to are suffocated in their Christian way of life by cares, riches, and pleasures, and do not advance to final maturity. This final maturity is seen as the persistent doing of good (8:15).[36] Luke also reports the conversion to Christianity of high-ranking and wealthy[37] sympathizers from the Jewish community (Acts 13:50; 17:12). Lydia also is a wealthy merchant (Acts 16:14–15). Already the Jesus movement in Palestine was supported financially by the wives of high-ranking men, according to Luke (8:3). A despised rich man—Zacchaeus, a "sinner" and chief tax collector (19:1–10)—serves as a model for the conduct of the rich. Those persons, too, may be presumed wealthy who consider their business more important than the invitation to the great banquet of God (14:16–24). Here, particularly, it becomes clear that Christians are addressed. And, finally, Luke counts nobles among those who confess the Christian faith, even though he does not use the term. The Roman governor of Cyprus, Sergius Paulus, who became a believer, might have been one of them (Acts 13:4–12);[38] also a certain Dionysius, a member of the Areopagus in Athens (Acts 17:34).

Conclusions About Social Stratification

If we disregard for a moment the Christians in Luke, then there were no rich *(plousioi)* or socially influential *(dynatoi)* members in the early Christian communities outside of Palestine. Unlike the Christians in Palestine, however, there were also no destitute *(ptōchoi)*. From the perspective of the rich and powerful, they were indeed poor *(penēs/asthenēs)* and powerless and of humble birth *(agenēs)*. Among them there were slaves, former slaves, freedmen (Philemon; 1 Cor. 7:21–24; see the list of greetings in Rom. 16:3–16), minor artisans (Paul, Prisca, and Aquila), merchants (James 4:13), and also, no doubt, day laborers. Some of them probably enjoyed the privileges of Roman citizenship *(civis Romanus*—Paul).[39] Some of them, without being of socially higher rank than the "poor" *(penēs)*, had their own slaves (Philemon) and oversaw a household *(oikos)* with servants. But this did not require socially and economically higher rank, as may be seen in the case of the Roman centurion Cornelius. He was a minor official among the Roman officers (Acts 10).[40] Furthermore, it should be noted that these Christians lived in small settled communities in contrast to those destitute Jewish followers of Jesus in Palestine. Yet they most certainly existed as marginal and endangered minorities, much like the Jewish synagogues of the Dispersion. Moreover, their external representation in relation to the outside world was more difficult than that of the Jewish synagogues which were recognized occasionally as organizations of "communities of exile" *(politeuma)*. One may legitimately assume that these Christian communities were seen as associations (clubs) by the surrounding society,[41] regardless of how they themselves might have perceived their community. Their gatherings were public (1 Corinthians 14; James 2:1–7), and with time there seems to have developed within the communities a practice of mutual assistance modeled after that of the synagogues. I cannot deal with this issue of intracommunal charity here nor with the significant role of women in the early Christian communities.[42]

The Poor and the Gospel of "The Little People"

The Intermediate Social Status of the Christian Poor

The intermediate social status of the Christian poor *(penētes)*, between the rich and powerful on the one hand and the utterly poor and powerless on the other, is reflected very nicely in the Letter of James. The line of argumentation in James 2:1–13 presupposes exactly this situation. On the one hand, James points out to his Christian audience that God has elected the destitute *(ptōchoi)* before the world as rich in faith, yet they have treated the poor with contempt. On the other hand, he reminds the Christians that it is the rich who oppress them, who drag them into the courts and blaspheme the name by which they are called (2:5–7). Whatever the specific incident to which James makes reference (2:6: "Yet you have dishonored the poor man."),[43] he is concerned in principle with a partisan attitude (2:1: "show no partiality" [*mē en prosō-polēmpsiais echete*]; see also 2:9) that prefers the rich and highly ranked over the destitute *(ptōchos)*. James calls this behavior a sin *(hamartia)* that breaks the whole Law *(nomos = Torah)*, because it breaks one commandment thereof, even though all other commandments were observed (2:9–11). Here he is probably alluding to Lev. 9:15: "You shall do no injustice in judgment; you shall not be partial to the poor or defer to the great, but in righteousness shall you judge your neighbor."

Is it possible that James is concerned here only with the incident described in 2:1–4, the contemptuous treatment of a poor person or the preferential treatment of a rich person in the assembly? In 2:1 it is said that one cannot have faith in Jesus Christ and "act in a partisan way" *(prosōpolēmpsiais,* plural). On the positive side, James then points to the "royal law" of the love of neighbor. This they shall obey, and thus do good.[44] And when finally he states that one who does not practice mercy *(mē poiēsanti eleos)* will not find mercy on the day of judgment, and that, on the other hand, mercy *(eleos)* will triumph over judgment (2:13), James is as concerned with *action* as he is with the *subject* of love of neighbor (see also 3:17, where James speaks of the "good fruits" [*karpoi agathoi*] of mercy). Thus, the author of the letter exhorts his readers to do good to the destitute *(ptōchoi),* and, furthermore, admonishes them to assess realistically their own situation with regard to the rich. Your "neighbors," he implies, are not the rich but the destitute whom God has chosen. The commandment to love the neighbor, accordingly, is interpreted here in terms of compassion for the very poor. That it is called *here*, of all places, the "royal law" *(nomos basilikos,* 2:8) would then make all the more sense since the poor are the ones who will inherit that "royal rule" *(basileia)* to which it belongs.

Their Critical Distance from the
Political Domain

The Gospel of Luke is no less critical in its distance from
the rich *(plousioi)* than the Letter of James. That is not our
concern here, however.[45] More widespread is a very *critical
stance over against the hierarchical order of government*—experienced on the political level as well as on the level
of the households *(oikos, oikia)* as economic and social units.[46]
Even in the New Testament we have examples of the similarity
of this differential of power on the large (state) and small
(household) scale (Mark 10:41–45; see also Matt. 20:24–28
and Luke 22:24–27). The Christians in the urban regions of
the Roman Empire were able to capitalize on the abuse of
government in the political realm as a model for charting an
antithetical social order in their own communities, keeping in
mind the circumstances of a "household."

Here I will discuss briefly the attitudes of these Christian
communities toward the state, leaving aside those texts that
are commonly referred to in this context (for example, Romans
13). Then I will attempt an explanation of the Christian alternative that is informed by the hierarchy of a "household."

Mark (and similarly, Matthew) very negatively characterizes
the political domain as a brutal subjugation *(katakyrieuein)* and
a misuse of office *(katexousiazein)*.[47] "You know that those
who are supposed to rule over the Gentiles lord it over them,
and their great men exercise authority over them" (Mark 10:42;
see also Matt. 20:25).[48] Ultimately it makes no difference whether
this is meant to be a general assertion concerning the rulers of
the individual peoples, which seems unlikely to me, or a specific statement about those who were the brutal conquerors of
most of the contemporary nations, namely, the Romans.[49]

In the parallel verse in Luke (22:25), one clearly detects the
ideology of government not only of the Hellenistic rulers but
also of the Roman Caesars: "The kings of the Gentiles exercise

lordship *(kyrieuousin)* over them; and those in authority over them are called benefactors" *(euergetai)*. Luke in no way defuses the negative formulation of the Markan model when he uses the verb "exercise lordship" *(kyrieuousin,* which implicitly recalls the noun *kyrios,* title of a ruler). Indeed, he accurately portrays the self-representation of the government of that time. In combination with the title "Benefactor" *(euergetēs),* which also belongs to the ideology of government, this is a likely interpretation. Here, too, we must ask whether Luke is generalizing or talking implicitly about the rule of the Roman Caesars. In any case, the latter cannot be ruled out since the titles of "Lord" *(kyrios)* and "Benefactor" *(euergetēs)* were bestowed on Roman emperors as well as on foreign and domestic vassals in the provinces.[50] Luke himself is familiar with the title *kyrios* for the Roman emperor (Acts 25:26). It may recall the *dominus* (= *kyrios)* as master of slaves,[51] as well as paraphrase the divinelike character of the emperor. Domitian, for instance, had himself worshiped as "Our Lord and God" *(dominus et deus noster).* It is precisely the claiming of *kyrios* for Jesus, as well as *sotēr* (savior = deliverer) and *archēgos* (leader),[52] that suggests an intentional challenge to Rome's ideology of government. In the eyes of Luke, the rule of the Caesars ultimately typifies an antithesis to the rule of God, namely, the "power of darkness" *(exousia tou skotous,* Luke 22:53; Acts 26:18). The rule of the Roman emperor over the inhabited world—*oikumenē* stands for the Roman Empire in Luke (see Luke 4:5 and Acts 11:28)—is made possible by the devil's bequest (Luke 4:5–8).[53]

Those Who Serve Attain the Highest Rank

Following their indictment of the political domain (Mark 10:42; Matt. 20:25; Luke 22:25), all three Synoptic Gospels contrast the misuse of political rule, through reference to a "household," with an *alternative practice* expected in the Christian community. Within the social order of a "household," it is not only the slave who is expected to render service to his master *(kyrios* and *oikodespotēs,* Luke 12:35–40) but also the youngest *(neōteros)* who is expected to serve the elder *(presbyteros),* who is therefore greater *(meizōn)* than he (see Acts 5:6, 10).

The "Christian" alternative, *according to Mark,* calls for a reversal of this power pyramid. The one who is or would be "the highest" *(megas, meizōn, prōtos)* in the Christian community is to be "the servant of all" *(pantōn diakonos),* or "slave of all" *(pantōn doulos;* see Mark 10:43–45; 9:35). Mark is concerned here not so much with low social status as such but rather with the disciples' performance of lowly social tasks. The paradigmatic case of such "serving" for Mark is taking in an uncared-for child (9:36–37; 10:13–16).[54] The servant task of the disciples, and evidently of those Christian contemporaries who served in leading positions, is interpreted by Mark "christologically": "For the Son of Man also came not to be served but to serve and to give his life as a ransom for many" (10:45).

In this context *Matthew* (18:1–5) is thinking more of a social abasement of the disciples/Christians. He positions them in the lowest level of societal consciousness and its practice: that of a small child *(paidion).*[55] The disciples are to become like these children, in the sense that they have an absolute lack of rights and power as well as social worth. In that way they will attain the highest rank in the royal rule of God.

Luke agrees with Matthew in that he takes the low social status of children as an example for the reversal of the conventional gradation of social esteem that is now operative in the Christian community (Luke 9:46–48, esp. 48c; 18:15–17; note the transition from 18:9–14). It is interesting that in this context, concerning social rank among Christians, Luke avoids a comparison with the subordinate relation of slaves to their master. In this respect he differs from Matthew and Mark. He sees the Christian community as a "household" of brothers. The greatest of them *(meizōn)* is to be as the youngest *(neōteros)*, the one who leads *(hēgoumenos)* as the one who serves *(diakonōn)* in the household (22:26). The term *hēgoumenos* in particular clearly demonstrates the parenetic intention of Luke [that is, to advise and counsel]: this intention concerns the leadership structure of the community (see Acts 15:22). I believe, therefore, that it is necessary to consider whether the term *presbyteros*, denoting "elders" in the community, might be understood, at least in Luke, from this context of social rank within a "household" (see Acts 14:23; 20:17). In such a household, however, there are now not slaves and masters but younger and older brothers (or sisters and brothers). Luke, too, provides a "christological" foundation for the servant role of the leading Christians. He is not referring, to be sure, to a fundamental statement about "the Son of Man as servant" but points to the example of Jesus serving the apostles during their last Passover meal together (Luke 22:14–27). For here Jesus fulfilled the socially lower function in relation to the apostles, waiting on them as they reclined at table (22:27). For the household of Christians as a whole, the axiom is: "Every one who exalts himself will be humbled, and he who humbled himself will be exalted" (14:11). Luke demonstrates this with the help of the Hellenistic *topos* of the banquet, a symbol of life itself. He uses the example of the Pharisee and the tax collector to explain his criticism of those who deem themselves righteous and despise others (18:9–14). In contrast to such persons stands the repentant sinner, in the person of the tax collector, whom they are to emulate. The tax collector stands for persons, like him, who are considered sinners and indeed are sinners.[56] The Pharisee in Luke is representative of Christians who regard their fellow Christians with contempt.[57] It is evident that even then Luke was confronted with the problem of differences in social value within his Christian community.

Solidarity with the Poor

The emphasis on serving *(diakonein)* among the Christian brothers and sisters has a direct relation to the formation of a highly developed solidarity with one another which prompted Adolf von Harnack's justifiable remark that "one may further describe the Christian preaching as *the preaching of love and charity.*"[58] Therefore, in an empire whose ideology of government was most sharply indicted by its own practice, it is extremely likely that the communal cohesiveness of these marginal groups was more appealing to the dependent and oppressed strata of society than to the rich and highly ranked who profited from this government. Another indication of the powerless minority status of the Christian poor *(penētes)* is the fact that they hardly entertained any notion of direct political confrontation with abusive rule (perhaps, in Romans 13 Paul alludes to actual tendencies of Christians toward civil disobedience). The arena for an alternative life style was in the communities themselves. Within them there gradually developed an *intracommunal, intra-Christian*, charitable activity. With its basis in Jewish models this activity came to be the hallmark of these Christians—through their care for widows, orphans, the sick, the needy, and those in prison as well as through their hospitality toward fellow believers passing through town. It is precisely this conduct for which the Christians commend each other (see the beginning of the *First Letter of Clement* to the Corinthians).

We are concerned, however, with Christian charity toward the destitute *(ptōchoi)* as it is documented in the New Testament. Assuming the thesis of the social composition of the earliest Christian communities outside Palestine advanced here, it is clear that we are *not* dealing with intra-Christian charitable practice. This is an important point since that is understandably the initial assumption on which the discussion of the diaconal activities of the early Christians proceeds. Moreover, the predominance of intra-Christian charitable activity over solidarity with non-Christians is reflected in many writings.[59]

While intra-Christian aid affects a broad spectrum of beneficiaries—widows, orphans, the sick, the needy, prisoners, even officials like missionaries and teachers—the destitute *(ptōchoi)* are the focal point of Christian compassion for non-Christians. Finally, the care for needy non-Christians is likely to have been a factor in the process of Christian self-identification. And this does not necessarily imply that the issue was consciously exploited for this purpose.[60] For it was precisely in this aid to the poorest of the poor that the Christians, and most likely also the Jews, differentiated themselves so clearly from their Western pagan contemporaries. Of course, Greeks and Romans, too, gave to the destitute, but not out of a sense of moral obligation; nor was such an act counted as charity, for among the recipients there is no mention of the *ptōchoi*.[61]

In order to appreciate the compassionate behavior of the early Christian community outside of Palestine, it is therefore important to realize that they considered assistance to the destitute one of their moral-religious obligations. It is unusual that not only did they give them alms but also they could and did explain this assistance within the context of their (religious) "morality." This, of course, reveals the origin of the Christian faith from Judaism. A further differentiation is necessary, however, for it is that specific Jewish tradition that has its historical and theological roots in the messianic Jesus movement of poor Palestinian Jews which made possible this particular course of events. It is the specific situation of the Christian poor *(penētes)* outside Palestine which transformed solidarity *among* the poor into solidarity *with* the poor.

In this context *Luke-Acts* is of particular significance. To begin with, it is striking how often Luke talks about the giving of alms, about charitable behavior toward the poor. In the speech against the Pharisees (Luke 11:37–44), he contrasts the rules of ritual purity with the call to donate the "contents" *(ta enonta)* of those purified vessels as alms to the poor (11:41). The intention here is not to criticize the Pharisees, which would in any case be untenable in this form, but rather to accentuate in a poignant way the giving of alms with a Christian audience in mind. This becomes clear later on in the text when the same challenge is issued to the disciples: they should sell their possessions and give them as alms (12:33). (This is hardly to be taken as a historical occurrence involving disciples of Jesus in Palestine, nor should the Pharisees here be historicized.)[62]

Acts 3:1–10 illustrates graphically the situation of a lame beggar who is asking for alms—in this case not gifts of money. He receives much more—his very health, in fact, and thereby presumably his ability to work. Acts 9:36–43 and 10:1–33 portray some exemplary almsgivers, Tabitha and the centurion Cornelius, in their resultant good fortune. For one thing, the Tabitha story indicates that alms may be pieces of clothing (under- and outer garments are shown to Peter).[63] At any rate, the primary thing about this "miracle story" is the interconnection between Tabitha's exemplary charity and her being raised up from the dead. I am inclined to see in this resurrection story a paradigmatic depiction of the destiny of those who, like Tabitha, strive to be "full of good works and acts of charity" (Acts 9:36). It is also Luke in particular who places special emphasis on the recompense for charity toward the poor at the resurrection. Thus, Luke justifies the renunciation of possessions demanded of the disciples with these words: they are to provide themselves "with a treasure in the heavens that does not fail" (12:33).[64] Luke, in particular, motivates charitable giving to the poor with a promise: "You will be repaid at the resurrection of the just" (14:14).

In the legend about the conversion of the centurion Cornelius that immediately follows the Tabitha incident, the many alms Cornelius gave to the people of Israel play an important role: they ascend for him, along with his prayers, as a memorial before God (Acts 10:4). Here, as well as in Acts 24:17, Israel is named as the beneficiary of the alms. This is a specific legitimation of the relationship between the almsgiver and the people of Israel.[65] Cornelius is presented, so to speak, as the "model pagan." He is a "god-fearer," not a proselyte, who maintains an intimate relationship with the synagogue, yet without having taken the final step of conversion to Judaism. (It would have been impossible for a Roman officer to take such a step without grave consequences for his life.) He thus belonged to that group of sympathizers with the Jewish synagogues which was to become, according to Acts, the chief source of new converts—especially distinguished women—to the Christian community. This is precisely the problematic which forms the background to this story; in other words, the story of Cornelius's conversion has an apologetic intent. He is presented as an exemplary "god-fearer" who is acceptable even in the eyes of the Jews. Regarding the alms given to Israel by Cornelius, one could easily think of good deeds like the gift of the centurion from Capernaum: he built a synagogue (Luke 7:5), yet it is also possible that he gave alms directly to the poor Jews.[66]

Besides Luke, only Matthew (6:2–4) employs the term "alms" (*eleēmosynē*). Matthew, however, is objecting to an *improper* practice of almsgiving which he basically presupposes among his addressees, who probably were predominantly Jewish Christians. Luke, on the other hand, is generally interested in encouraging the practice of almsgiving—building upon a very lax and insignificant practice, at best, and wishing to invigorate it. Luke 14:12–14 clearly shows that the author of this Gospel attributes a Hellenistic social morality to his readers, probably predominantly gentile Christians. To this Hellenistic morality

Luke adds his own special concern for the destitute *(ptōchoi):* here, hospitality—the friendly interaction of peers—is applied to the poor. Instead of inviting friends, brothers, relatives, and rich neighbors to the banquet, one is to ask the poor, the crippled, the lame, and the blind to the meal. Such a host to the poor may then expect from God the recompense *(anta-podoma)* that ordinarily could be expected from one's peers, which, thereby in fact would exclude the poor from this social activity. Such a host will be repaid at the resurrection of the just. Moreover, Luke uses this same Christian interpretation *(interpretatio christiana)* of Hellenistic social morality with respect to intracommunal charitable activity. The interpretation of the original community in Jerusalem in terms of the Greco-Roman ideal of a community of friends *(koinōnia tōn philōn)* in Acts 2 and 4 is particularly striking. But no more on that here.[67]

Apart from the texts discussed here, it must be pointed out that Luke wants to see the rich not merely renounce their possessions but use them in the service of the destitute *(ptō-choi).* In Luke 18:18–22 the rich ruler, upon being asked to sell his possessions and distribute them to the poor, fails to achieve that which the rich chief tax collector Zacchaeus accomplishes. The latter wants to donate half of his possessions to the poor (see Luke 18:22 and 19:8). This behavior is remarkable particularly in the context of the Cynic tradition of renunciation of possessions. For, in the Cynic tradition, ultimately the renunciation itself remains the critical achievement of the one who renounces; the *use* of one's possessions is up to the individual's imagination. The poor, in any case, are not the intended recipients. Conversely, it must be noted that Luke never commends poverty itself as an exemplary state (for its independence, for example); he commends only the disciples who have voluntarily become poor in their following Jesus. The call to renounce possessions, therefore, is not the expression of an ascetic ideal. Rather, it is, on the one hand, an appreciation of the disciples' renunciation resulting from their following Jesus. On the other hand, it is an indictment of the rich and an expression of solidarity with the poor. It merely needs to be pointed out that Luke envisioned charitable solidarity with the poor as the task of individual Christians, not as a community task.

From all appearances, the author of Luke-Acts seems to be directing exhortations concerning assistance to the destitute primarily to wealthy Christians. This is evident, above all, from the intimate link between the call for renunciation of possessions and assistance to the poor (again, Luke 18:22 and 19:8). Yet it is obvious that Luke fully expects less well-to-do Christians also to support the poor. We do not know the exact financial situation of either the exemplary Tabitha or the centurion Cornelius, but it is unlikely that they were rich. Cornelius held a low rank in the Roman hierarchy of officers, and Acts 9:39 implies that Tabitha herself made garments. The argument of Luke 11:41 ("give for alms those things which are within") refers to relatively moderate alms. Luke 3:11 even reckons with solidarity among the destitute themselves: "He who has two coats, let him share with him who has none; and he who has food, let him do likewise." Probably, everyone is to give according to their own ability, that is, according to their financial status, as is implied in a different context—that of mutual assistance between Christian communities (Acts 11:29–30). Paul refers the elders from Ephesus to the example of his own behavior: they, too, should support their missionary work by their own labor and care for the weak. He refers here to otherwise unknown words of Jesus: "It is more blessed to give than to receive" (Acts 20:33–35).

Beyond these concrete guidelines for assistance to the poor, Luke—one might call him the first theologian—sketches a "theology of the poor." His portrayal of Jesus' ministry and

of the discipleship of his first followers presents the Jesus
movement as a movement of the poor. Luke combines those
few remarks that he could adopt from the Gospel of Mark with
a tradition from the ''Sayings Source'' to outline a history of
Jesus and his disciples in Palestine in which voluntary poverty
on the part of the disciples contrasts sharply with the rich. This
intention is clearly expressed in the contrast between the ''beatitude of the poor'' *(ptōchoi* refers here to the disciples of Jesus
in Luke 6:20–23) and the ''woe over the rich'' in 6:24–26.
The Magnificat of Mary (Luke 1:46–55) already celebrates the
expected reversal of the fortunes of the lowly and the rich
(1:52–53). And it is Luke in particular who frequently stresses
the fact that the gospel is preached to the poor (4:18; 7:22).
Many of Jesus' miracles of healing occurred in such a milieu
(4:31–44; 5:12–26; 6:6–11). Aside from the poor and the sick,
it is the sinners who are addressed as beneficiaries of Jesus'
mission during his earthly activity. Of course, Luke can no
longer imagine that Jesus and his first followers in Palestine
did not have to become poor voluntarily, but that they shared
quite involuntarily the lot of many of their Jewish compatriots.
Luke describes the explicit *renunciation of possessions* by the
disciples (see 5:11), but his presentation of Jesus' childhood
(Luke 2) in no way suggests that his parents were among the
poor; we only know that they traveled to Jerusalem every year
for the Passover feast (2:41). And yet he does not hesitate to
present the Jesus movement *as* a movement of the poor. Jesus
himself does not seem to have had any possessions since Luke
mentions the support of the Jesus movement by high-ranking
women (8:3). On the contrary, these ''virtues'' of Jesus and
his followers are converted by Luke into a sharp indictment of
the rich; his affection for the rejected becomes a pointed indictment of the respected. In antiquity only the ''authentic''
Cynic itinerant philosophers, not their imitators in the salons
of the rich, had directed the criticism of their own destitution

and frugal existence with similar bluntness against the luxurious life of the rich. Yet Luke points not to a frugal, alternative life style but to an alternative to the destitution of the poor and the luxurious life of the rich. This alternative is a balance between the two. He imagines this very simply, as demonstrated by the story of the rich chief tax collector Zacchaeus: the rich forego half of their possessions (Luke 19:8; see the interesting parallel 3:11 as a standard of solidarity among the poor themselves). This ideal balance was at least realized for a short time among the Christians themselves, in the earliest community in Jerusalem: "They had everything in common," and "there was not a needy person among them" (Acts 4:32–37; see also 2:43–47).

One further thing should be mentioned in this connection: Paul's formal "collection" to assist the poor among the "saints" in Jerusalem (see Rom. 15:26) must be understood as an act of solidarity of the poor (here *penētes)* with those even poorer *(ptōchoi)*. This collection also envisions a balance which creates community *(koinōnia)*: the people of Jerusalem, through their thanksgiving to God, restore what other Christians had donated in supply of their want (2 Cor. 9:11–14).

Prosperous Christians and the Gospel of the Poor

Summary

It should be noted that in the foregoing analysis of New Testament texts I established the sociohistorical correlation of these texts as a criterion for their understanding. For the interpretation of the verses discussed, the living conditions which are addressed and in which the "authors" and/or "addressees" found themselves are of crucial significance. The actual details, of course, are difficult to reconstruct. They can be inferred, however, to a degree which permits a sociohistorical understanding of the texts.

In the first stage I identified a "phenomenology" of the destitute *(ptōchoi)*, so to speak, as it is discernible in the appropriate passages. The *ptōchoi* are destitute, sick, poorly clothed, and dependent on others for the basic necessities, for which they must beg. This characterization of the destitute is common to all of antiquity; it is not confined to Palestine. What is important is the fact that the New Testament texts do not use the term *penēs* to characterize the poor. They use the exact term for utter poverty *(ptōchoi)*, and, indeed, that is what is meant. Thus, the New Testament texts seem to reflect a social situation in which the number of these beggars has increased significantly compared, for instance, to the conditions in the

Greek cities of preceding centuries. But it is clear that the texts also have a special interest in the poor.

In the second stage of my investigation, I attempted to assign the texts under discussion more precisely to the sociohistorical situations of their "authors" and/or "addressees," according to the texts' specific focus on poverty. In the process I distinguished between two distinct approaches to the problem of poverty, which can be defined according to temporal, geographical, and literary criteria as well as according to the social conditions of their "representative groups."

According to my presentation, the first- and second-generation followers of Jesus in Palestine were destitute. They saw themselves as the subjects of the history of salvation of Israel's God with his people, and they practiced solidarity among themselves. The Christian communities in the urban regions of the Roman Empire beyond Palestine did not include the destitute (*ptōchoi*), according to my characterization. These communities consisted predominantly of "the little people" (*penētes*), who not only strove for solidarity among themselves but also developed an awareness of the problems of those poor (non-Christians) who were even more needy than themselves and whom they felt duty bound to assist. This bond with the poorest of the poor takes on special significance in the situation of the Lukan Christians whose community already included some wealthy members. For Luke, as well as for Matthew (see Matt. 25:31–46), this bond has a direct relation to the Christians' credal convictions and must not be isolated from these as mere "ethical" consequence.

Revelations in the Life of the Faithful

The reader may disagree with certain aspects of the interpretation advanced here. I am concerned, however, with the general intention of the whole. I read the New Testament as a

monument to the *faith and life* of the earliest Christian groups
and communities within and beyond Palestine. I do not thereby
overlook the fact that all New Testament texts are united by
the *faith* in the saving revelation of God in Jesus Christ—however
that faith may have been expressed. *For, this faith cannot be
divorced from the life of the faithful.* It becomes palpable, and
therefore more meaningful, precisely by its relation to the believers' particular living conditions. Even the preaching of
Jesus becomes plain only in its relation to his activity and his
life, and its defined circumstances, and to the life of his first
followers in Palestine. We cannot understand the faith in Jesus
Christ unless we learn to grasp it from the sociohistoric situation
of the believers themselves. Bartimaeus, and all those figures
of misery who could identify with his plight, not only believed
in Jesus of Nazareth, Son of David, as a historical person
representing the eschatological King of Israel but he, and they,
also experienced Jesus as the one who shows mercy even to
the miserable. For Bartimaeus and for those who tell of the
miraculous transformation of his life of misery, the point is
not merely that they believe in a historical person as the Mes-
siah/King. Rather, this faith, and the hope which it inspires
is in its content—almost programmatically—the faith and hope
of the poor. Therefore, understanding the life situation of the
believers is not a means of explaining how these people, as a
result of their circumstances, "projected" their hopes onto a
certain person (Jesus) as a godsent savior. Instead, it permits
us to understand concretely their faith in the saving revelation
of God in Jesus Christ.

This is true not only of the Palestine followers of Jesus but
also of those Christians in the urban regions of the Roman
Empire who—out of their own situation and with their own
theological agenda—then believed in Jesus Christ as the saving
revelation of God. If, therefore, the primary interest in New
Testament exegesis is *theological*, namely, the attempt to un-

derstand God's saving revelation in Jesus Christ, then socio-historical exegesis, understood in that way, is also theological. Sociohistorical exegesis reads the New Testament as a monument to the *faith and life* of those people who, from the earliest beginnings of the Jesus movement, bear witness to their faith in the saving revelation of God in Jesus Christ.

Thus, the New Testament for me bears witness to this revelation insofar as it is witness to the *faith* in this revelation manifested in the "confession" and life style of the believers. And, of course, we have this revelation of God in Jesus Christ only in these earthen vessels. The New Testament is not itself this revelation of God; the Christian faith is not a "religion of the book." Rather, it is a historical movement that originated in Palestinian Judaism at the beginning of the Common Era. In its "founding charter"—the Bible—this movement recounts, in the Old Testament, the history of God with his people as the history of this people with its God. In the New Testament it records the continuation of this history in, with, and under the history of those who believe in Jesus Christ as the saving revelation of God to Israel and to the nations. In the canon of the Bible this historical movement of Christians has established its roots in the history of Israel and the account of its own origin. In any given moment, therefore, this Christian movement understands itself against that background, and by that standard it measures itself and must be measured by others. Thus, reading the Bible is also an act of ascertaining whether Christianity continues in the tradition of discipleship to Jesus.

Our Affluence Demands a Sociohistorical Exegesis

Within the conditions of *our* sociohistoric situation and that of contemporary Christianity, moreover, a *historical* understanding of the biblical tradition seems to me helpful and nec-

essary. We have to inquire into the self-understanding of those
Christians who are heard in the New Testament. We have to
ask who they were and under what conditions of social, economic, political, cultural, and religious life their faith in Jesus
Christ found its particular expression. We have to ask these
questions not only because we are separated from these early
Christians by time or even by enormous scientific advances.
To use Rudolf Bultmann's familiar words of demythologiza-
tion, ''We live in the era of electric lights.'' These are necessary
questions because our existence is so determined by the material conditions of our life that we will only misunderstand
the biblical texts unless we appreciate the historical distance
separating us from these texts and the world they portray.

When, on the other hand, ''the little people'' in Solentiname,
El Salvador, or the Philippines read the Gospels, they learn
something about themselves. They are not separated from the
tradition of discipleship to Jesus inside or beyond the Palestine
of that time by the ''loathsome gulf'' of history. The biblical
traditions reflect substantially the same reality of hunger and
poverty, oppression and violence that they encounter daily in
the flesh. Critical self-examination should tell us, therefore,
that the following sarcastic remarks by Søren Kierkegaard are
also aimed at us:

> In the magnificent cathedral the Honorable and Right Reverend
> Geheime-General-Oberhof-Prädikant, the elect favorite of the
> fashionable world, appears before an elect company and preaches,
> with emotion, upon the text which he himself elected: ''God
> hath elected the base things of the world and the things that are
> despised''—and nobody laughs.[68]

Thus, it is the real gap between our living conditions and
those of the early Christians which demands a historically concrete interpretation of the Bible: interpreters must *substantially*
deal with the gap between the satisfied and the hungry, the
rich and the poor—together with everything that determines

the life of the wealthy *(plousioi)* and the destitute *(ptōchoi)* in this day and age! And insofar as this gap continues today to separate us from a great host of hungry and poor people in this world, it is a distance not only in theory but in fact, not only in history but at this moment. Therefore, in the interest of discipleship to Jesus Christ, a sociohistorical interpretation of the biblical texts is a theologically necessary way to read the Bible. In any case, this holds true for affluent Christians. It is not possible for us to perceive the saving revelation of God in Jesus Christ (the task of theology as I see it) *in isolation from the way in which it was manifested concretely in time and space.* Faith in the Messiah, Christian faith, is more than the *faithful* identification of one person as the Messiah/Christ; it is also an identification with the program represented by this person. This was true from the very beginning of the messianic movement connected with the name of Jesus, among those who agreed with it as well as those who opposed it. What constituted messianism was not the fact that here people believed and followed one as the Messiah/Christ but rather which *preaching* and which *practice* of this person, in a messianic sense, was acclaimed (or denied). Jesus of Nazareth himself, the proclaimer who has become the proclaimed, draws into the kerygma all those who were the focus of his message and ministry, who, within their circumstances and responsibilities, could and did express their hopes through his person. Nor can he today be perceived, believed, and proclaimed by us apart from them. Not even the poor, wretched, and despised people of Israel, whom he invited to a hope-filled future in the kingdom of God, are incidental extras in the unfathomable will of God to let his Word become flesh. Indeed, these "little people" and their God belong together; they are bearers and recipients alike of this Word of which they are a constituent part and which has assumed concrete form as the "gospel of the poor" *(ptōchoi euaggelizontai:* Luke 7:22; see also Matt. 11:5 and

Luke 4:18). Thus, the point here is not the old problem of the "historical Jesus" but rather the concretization of the revelation of God in his Messiah. We can speak of this revelation only by speaking also of its "manifest" content, the gospel of the poor. Ernst Käsemann, at the World Mission Assembly in Melbourne (1980), put it this way:

> The king of the heavenly realm continues to travel the streets of this world. One has comprehended nothing about him if one seeks him in the wrong places and proclaims him under false slogans. He can be found always and only in places where redemption is needed, that is, according to Ps. 107:10, among those who sit "in darkness and gloom, prisoners in affliction and in irons."[69]

Justification—A False Understanding

We affluent Christians, therefore, can no longer deal with the "good news" the way Freudian psychoanalysis deals with dreams. Thus, as though the "manifest" content of revelation contains only the accidental historical material, Christian theology spares no pains in order to discover the "essential core," the hidden content of this revelation. This plumbing of the "depths" must necessarily lead to extremely abstract insights by means of which the "gospel for the poor" could then become the gospel for the rich. Such psychoanalysis would insist, for instance, that rich and poor are equally guilty before God, that the "good news" applies to both equally.[70] It plays off, one might say, a false understanding of Paul's theology of justification against the kerygma of the Gospels.

I would like to illustrate this with the help of a reinterpretation of the parable of the Pharisee and the tax collector (Luke 18:9–14). The parable needs only to be altered slightly, namely, in good Lutheran-Pauline tradition it would have to tell of a wealthy Christian who no longer points with pride to his or

her religious "achievements" but confesses their sinfulness
before God. Of course, one would immediately include the
pauper beside oneself in the confession of guilt and accuse him
of being a sinner also. The master accuses the servant of a
similar abstract sinfulness instead of repenting of his own sin
and refraining from sinning in the future by directly or indi-
rectly participating in the pauperization of his servant. This
treatment of rich and poor, master and slave, as equal in relation
to sin, is itself sin "before God," since "before the world"
it is paralleled by an often cruel reality of nonequality. In actual
fact, it amounts to a self-justification of the sinner. Particularly
we Christians in Western industrialized countries have to be-
ware of creating a false distinction between the message of
justification and the gospel of the poor. Though there be differences between the two, they should not be played off against
each other! We must live with the tension and see the impos-
sibility of our saying "We belong to Paul" while the Christians
in the poor countries of this world say "We belong to the
Messiah of the poor." Is Christ then divided?

Make Friends for Yourselves by Means of
Unrighteous Mammon

A truly historical understanding of the good news neither
separates the saving revelation of God in Jesus Christ from the
people who believed it back then nor does it separate the faith
of those people from their life and the circumstances deter-
mining it. Such an understanding will then discover in the
gospel not only those things that separate us from the tradition
of discipleship but also *the opportunities and possibilities that
reconcile us to the gospel* and place us within the tradition of
the Messiah of the poor from Nazareth. It offers us, too, the
possibility of beginning the true life within the false, of learning
to hope.

Among many examples, I find one particularly appropriate: the parable of the unjust steward (Luke 16:1–13). The parable tells of a rich man's steward, the slave[71] who managed the financial affairs of the rich man *(oikonomos)*. Because he has apparently embezzled certain moneys, he has to open the books. And he fears that he might lose his position and be forced to support himself as a farm laborer or lead the destitute life of a beggar.[72] Yet he cleverly doctors the promissory notes so as to obligate the debtors, hoping they will receive him into their houses. And "house" here means not simply shelter, but inclusion within a household as an economic and social unit. Jesus draws a conclusion from the parable for his disciples (v. 9): "And I tell you, make friends for yourselves by means of unrighteous mammon, so that when it fails they may receive you into the eternal habitations."[73] Luke's intention with this passage is to indicate that there is a legitimate use of money for the disciples that is *not* service of mammon: namely, to use it to make "friends" for themselves. Luke here picks up a Hellenistic *topos* concerning the "love of friends," which he alters to fit his theological intention. In classical antiquity, the making of friends in general reckons with repayment here and now in times of personal need, as exemplified by the conduct of the steward in the parable. By contrast, the Christian charitable practice which Luke has in mind here expects such repayment in the future life.[74] With impermanent mammon one may purchase permanent treasures (Luke 12:33).[75] The concluding phrases (16:13: "No servant can serve two masters," and "You cannot serve God and mammon") do not actually constitute a warning against the service of mammon, but rather point out once more that the disciples are not serving "mammon" when they use it to win friends.[76]

⋎   The important thing, therefore, is to use "mammon" wisely. Just as the rich chief tax collector gave half of what he owned to the poor *(ptōchoi,* Luke 19:1–10) here, too, unrighteous mammon should be used for doing good. Yet, the wealthy grain farmer dies because he accumulates riches for himself but is not rich toward God (Luke 12:13–21). He does not use his record harvest for a good purpose, he fails to purchase with it an "imperishable treasure."

Conclusion

Therefore, we affluent Christians, too, can make friends for ourselves by means of unrighteous mammon. We can become poorer in a purposeful way by giving away part of our wealth to benefit the poorest people of this world. Obviously, more is needed than such often helpful work as that of the Bread for the World organization. What is required is a contribution by the rich nations to the poor that impinges upon the substance of our accustomed standard of living and with it the carefully balanced equilibrium of societal interests. For only in that way, as all experts agree, a real change in the miserable situation of millions of people is possible.

Ultimately, only a change in the structure of the political and economic causes of the scandalous differential between rich and poor nations in this world can effect true help. We are a long way off from that. Yet, the successful application of this insight depends in part on the behavior of Christians, and especially on the influence and actions of the churches. I believe that in this context the story of the "widow's mite" (Luke 21:1–4; see also Mark 12:41–44) designates the task of the Christians. We affluent Christians of the West must recognize ourselves in the rich people of this story. Compared to the widow, we have placed much into the treasury for the poor. Of course, this contribution is worth little, since we have given of our surplus and not of our substance as did the poor widow. Yet that is what is justly required of us, for only such a substantial contribution, with today's insight we might add, can actually reverse the need and is therefore needful.

This task will catch on among Christians only when the churches as entire bodies act in that way—when they examine their budgets with a view to possible and called-for savings in order that a real share of the churches' budgets may go to the poor. For this to happen, there obviously must be a conversion of our theology and proclamation. We must learn to understand that the "theology of the poor" is becoming a central theme of theology in our times.[77] The relationship of Christians, churches, and theologians to global poverty no longer concerns merely Christianly self-evident charitable practice: it is becoming, rather, a question of Christian self-understanding. At issue is not merely a practical *consequence* of our faith in the saving revelation of God in Jesus Christ; *at issue is this faith itself*. The parable of the great judgment in Matt. 25:31–46 indicates the direction: our relationship to the poor of this world and our relationship to Jesus Christ, the Son of Man, are one and the same thing. For us wealthy Christians, a "theology of the poor" means that we must let our theological reflection be informed by the scandal of worldwide poverty, and that we not act any longer as if God has chosen the rich of this world.

Notes

1. For basic information regarding *ptōchoi*, *penētes*, and *plousioi*, see the entries in G. Kittel and G. Friedrich, ed., *Theological Dictionary of the New Testament* 6 (Grand Rapids: Wm. B. Eerdmans, 1968) and the cited literature.

2. See H. Bolkenstein, *Wohltätigkeit und Armenpflege im vorchristlichen Altertum* (Utrecht, 1939; Groningen, 1967), 184, 410.

3. Compare with Plato, *Crito* 53A.

4. Below are listed some of the works that deal specifically with socioeconomic conditions:

S. Appelbaum, "Economic Life in Palestine," in *The Jewish People in the First Century*, Compendia Rerum Iudaicarum ad Novum Testamentum (Philadelphia: Fortress Press; Assen, Netherlands: Van Gorcum, 1974), 2: 631–700.

F. C. Grant, *The Economic Background of the Gospels* (London: Oxford University Press, 1926).

M. Hengel, *Die Zeloten: Untersuchungen zur jüdischen Freiheitsbewegung*, 2d ed. (Leiden: E. J. Brill, 1976).

J. Jeremias, *Jerusalem in the Time of Jesus* (Philadelphia: Fortress Press; London: SCM Press, 1969).

H. G. Kippenberg, *Religion und Klassenbildung im antiken Judäa* (Göttingen: Vandenhoeck & Ruprecht, 1978).

H. Kreissig, *Die sozialen Zusammenhänge des judäischen Krieges* (East Berlin, 1970).

A. Schalit, *König Herodes: der Mann und sein Werk* (Berlin: Walter De Gruyter, 1969).

L. Schottroff and W. Stegemann, *Jesus von Nazareth—Hoffnung der Armen* (Stuttgart: Kohlhammer, 1978), 26–28 (English translation forthcoming from Orbis Books).

G. Theissen, "Wir haben alles verlassen (Mk. 10:28)," *Novum Testamentum* 19 (1977): 161ff.

5. John Chrysostom, *Homily on Matthew 18:21,* LX1.3. English translation in Nicene and Post-Nicene Fathers (Grand Rapids: Wm. B. Eerdmans, 1951), X:377–78. Luise Schottroff brought this text to my attention. See also Philo, *On the Special Laws* I.143; II.96; III.162–63.

6. Kreissig, *Die sozialen Zusammenhänge,* 119.

7. H. G. Kippenberg, *Religion und Klassenbildung,* 148.

8. See G. Dahlmann, *Orte und Wege Jesu* (Darmstadt, 1967); and "The Edicts of Diocletian VII" (English translation in *Roman Civilization Source Book II: The Empire,* ed. N. Lewis and M. Reinhold [New York: Harper & Row Torchbooks, 1966], 468).

9. Eusebius, *Ecclesiastical History* III.20.1–7. English translation by K. Lake. Vol. 1 of 2 vols. Loeb Classical Library (Cambridge: Harvard University Press; London: William Heinemann, 1926), 237–39.

10. Chrysostom, *Homily on Matthew 20:29–30,* LXVI.2

11. Regarding Mark 2:23–28, see L. Schottroff and W. Stegemann, "The Sabbath Was Made for Man: An Interpretation of Mark 2:23–28" in *God of the Lowly: Socio-Historical Interpretations of the Bible,* ed. W. Schottroff and W. Stegemann (Maryknoll, N.Y.: Orbis Books, 1984), 118–28. (This is an English translation by Matthew J. O'Connell from the German original *Der Gott der kleinen Leute,* 2 vols. [Munich: Chr. Kaiser, 1979].)

12. Josephus, *Jewish War* VII.437–50; see also the actions of the Egyptian false prophet, *Jewish War* II.261–63.

13. *Jewish War* VI.300–309: Josephus reports on the persecution of an uneducated prophet of doom, one Jesus Ben Ananias, against whom prestigious citizens had brought charges with the governor Albinus, and who barely escaped crucifixion despite his innocuousness.

14. Regarding the Magnificat, see L. Schottroff, "Das Magnificat und die älteste Tradition über Jesus von Nazareth," *Evangelische Theologie* 38 (1978): 298ff.

15. W. Wuellner, "The Sociological Implications of I Corinthians 1:26–28 Reconsidered," *Studia Evangelica* 4 (1973): 666–72 [= Texte und Untersuchungen 112].

16. E. A. Judge, *The Social Pattern of the Christian Groups in the First Century: Some Prolegomena to the Study of New Testament Ideas of Social Obligation* (London: Tyndale Press, 1960), 59–60.

17. Ibid., 60.

18. G. Theissen, "Social Stratification in the Corinthian Community: A Contribution to the Sociology of Early Hellenistic Christianity," in *The Social Setting of Pauline Christianity: Essays on Corinth,* edited and translated and with an Introduction by John H. Schütz (Philadelphia: Fortress Press; Edinburgh: T. & T. Clark, 1982), 69–119.

19. H. Kreissig ("Zur sozialen Zusammensetzung der frühchristlichen Gemeinden im ersten Jahrhundert u. Z.," *Eirene 6* [1967]: 91ff.) unfortunately knows nothing of the significance of the Synoptic Gospels for the solution to the problem posed in his essay.

20. See also Christoph Burchard, "Gemeinde in der strohernen Epistel: Mutmaszungen über Jacobus," in *Kirche* (Festschrift für Günther Bornkamm), ed. D. Lührmann and G. Strecker (Tübingen: J. C. B. Mohr [Paul Siebeck], 1980), 315ff., esp. 323–24.

21. Regarding the line of thought of the Letter of James, see Christoph Burchard, "Zu Jakobus 2:14–26," *Zeitschrift für die neutestamentliche Wissenschaft* 71 (1980): 27ff.

22. See L. Schottroff and W. Stegemann, *Jesus von Nazareth,* 129–36.

23. See H. J. Degenhardt, *Lukas Evangelist der Armen* (Stuttgart: Katholisches Bibelwerk, 1965). [Compare with Luke T. Johnson, *The Literary Function of Possessions in Luke-Acts* (Missoula, Mont.: Scholars Press, 1977)—for scholars; idem, *Sharing Possessions: Mandate and Symbol of Faith* (Philadelphia: Fortress Press, 1981)—for general readers; and with Walter E. Pilgrim, *Good News to the Poor* (Minneapolis: Augsburg Publishing House, 1981)—for general readers.]

24. This term (*katadynasteuein*) signifies a misuse of power. See the *Letter of Aristeas*; Diodorus Siculus, *History* XIII.73.

25. See Philo, *Against Flaccus* 57. See also V. Tcherikover, *Hellenistic Civilization and the Jews* (Philadelphia: Jewish Publication Society, 1959), 338 and throughout.

26. See Theissen, "Social Stratification," 234: "If Paul says that there were not many in the Corinthian congregation who were wise, powerful, and wellborn, then this much is certain: there were some."

27. Josephus, *Jewish War* VI.113–14; see also I.522.

28. The Vulgate translation, consequently, calls him an *arcarius civitatis*. See Theissen, "Social Stratification," 76. H. J. Cadbury ("Erastus of Corinth," *Journal of Biblical Literature* 50 [1931]: 42–58) considers him to be a slave.

29. Theissen, "Social Stratification," 73–83.

30. In this context, see Theissen's comprehensive and detailed presentation in "Social Stratification," 69–119.

31. See Plato, *Republic* II.364B.

32. See Plato, *Laches* 186C; Philo, *On the Virtues* 162.

33. See also W. Stegemann, "Vagabond Radicalism in Early Christianity? A Historical and Theological Discussion of a Thesis Proposed by Gerd Theissen," in *God of the Lowly*, 148–68, esp. 157–60 on Mark 10:28–30. Regarding the Lukan interpretation, see L. Schottroff and W. Stegemann, *Jesus von Nazareth*, 97–102. H. W. Kuhn ("Nachfolge nach Ostern," in *Kirche*, 105ff., esp. 125–26) questions my interpretation of Mark 10:28–30 as referring to "resident converts." He sees them as "itinerant missionaries."

34. Regarding the situation of the Markan Christians, see L. Schottroff, "Die Gegenwart in der Apokalyptik der synoptischen Evangelien," in *Apocalypticism in the Mediterranean World and the Near East,* ed. David Hellholm, Proceedings of the International Colloquium on Apocalypticism: Uppsala, August 12–17, 1979 (Tübingen: J. C. B. Mohr [Paul Siebeck], 1983), 707–28. See also my remarks in "Lasset die Kinder zu mir kommen. Sozial-geschichtliche Aspekte des Kinderevangeliums," in *Traditionen der Befreiung: Methodische Zugänge,* ed. W. Schottroff and W. Stegemann (Munich: Chr. Kaiser, 1980), 1:114–44 (English translation forthcoming from Fortress Press).

35. See L. Schottroff, "Human Solidarity and the Goodness of God: The Parables of the Workers in the Vineyard," in *God of the Lowly,* 129–47, esp. 139–42 on Matt. 19:16—20:28.

36. See the more detailed discussion on Luke 8:14 in L. Schottroff and W. Stegemann, *Jesus von Nazareth,* 120–22.

37. On "honest," "orderly," "becoming," see H. Greeven, "euschēmōn," *Theological Dictionary of the New Testament 2* (1964): 770–72.

38. See Judge, *Social Pattern,* 52–53.

39. See Pliny, *Epistles* X.96.4.

40. See also Judge, *Social Pattern,* 35. Even "the little people" could be slave owners. In this context, see S. S. Bartchy, *First Century Slavery and I Corinthians 7:21* (Missoula, Mont.: Scholars Press, 1973), 37ff. For Egypt, see the vivid description in E. Brunner-Traut, *Die alten Ägypter: Verborgenes Leben unter Pharaonen* (Stuttgart, 1976²), 202ff.

41. See Pliny, *Epistles* X.96.7.

42. Concerning Christian charity, see Adolf von Harnack, *The*

Mission and Expansion of Christianity in the First Three Centuries (New York: Harper & Row, 1962); and H.-J. Degenhardt, *Lukas—Evangelist der Armen*. Concerning the role of women, see L. Schottroff, "Frauen in der Nachfolge Jesu in neutestamentlicher Zeit," in *Traditionen der Befreiung: Frauen in der Bibel*, 2:91–133 (English translation forthcoming from Fortress Press). Regarding organizational forms of the Christian communities, see R. L. Wilken, "Collegia, Philosophical Schools, and Theology," in *The Catacombs and the Colosseum: The Roman Empire as the Setting of Primitive Christianity*, ed. S. Benko and J. J. O'Rourke (Valley Forge, Pa.: Judson Press, 1971), 268–91.

43. The case described in James 2:1–4 is perhaps a hypothetical exaggeration like the one concerning poor Christians in 2:14–16, possibly intended to illustrate graphically the improper *prosōpolēmpsia*. The *anēr chrysodaktylios en esthēti lampra* (2:2), whom Burchardt pointedly calls "Goldfinger" (*Kirche*, 322), might indeed signify a nobleman from the order of knights (*ordo equestris*, as suggested by the ring). See Judge, *Social Pattern*, 53. That he is rich is never stated, yet seems abundantly clear from the context. The addressees of James treat with respect those who oppress them (2:6, such as "Goldfinger"), but the poor, whom God has chosen, they treat with contempt, as for instance the poor man in the assembly.

44. Surely, the formulation *kalōs poieite* must be translated as "to do good," rather than "to act right" in the sense of "to do the proper thing." Concerning James 2:8, see also Luke 6:27. James 1:27 refers to an intracommunal act of charity.

45. See L. Schottroff and W. Stegemann, *Jesus von Nazareth*, 113–36.

46. With regard to *oikonomia* and its parallel application to the organization of the state, see the concise, but instructive, chapter on "The Household Community: Oikonomia," in Judge's *The Social Pattern*, 30–39.

47. For the negative terms used here, see W. Bauer, *A Greek-English Lexicon of the New Testament and Other Early Christian Literature* (Chicago: University of Chicago Press, 1979), under the respective entries.

48. In my opinion, the formulation *hoi dokountes archein* (Mark 10:42) refers, to begin with, only to the genuine task of "governing." It is not limited in this sense chiefly in principle, rather through the misuse of office referred to in my comments on Mark.

49. In this context, see the statement of the Britannic commander in chief, Calgacus, in Tacitus's piece on his father-in-law, Agricola (*Agricola* 30.4):

> Robbers of the world, having by their universal plunder exhausted the land, they rifle the deep. If the enemy be rich, they are rapacious; if he be poor, they lust for dominion; neither the east nor the west has been able to satisfy them. Alone among men they covet with equal eagerness poverty and riches. To robbery, slaughter, plunder, they give the lying name of empire (*imperium*); they make a solitude and call it peace (*pax*).

(The English translation is from *The Complete Works of Tacitus* [New York: The Modern Library, 1942], 695.) The inhabited world (*orbis terrarum oikumenē*) is in fact a mass of slaves bullied by the Romans.

50. See *Against Flaccus* 74.126; *On the Embassy to Gaius* 22. The writings concerning the cult of the ruler, or Caesar, are legion. Here I mention only the important monograph by K. Scott, *The Imperial Cult under the Flavians* (Stuttgart/Berlin: Kohlhammer, 1936). [On social, economic, and political factors in the Gospel of Luke, one should consult the works of Frederick W. Danker: *Benefactor: Epigraphic Study of a Graeco-Roman and New Testament Field* (St. Louis: Clayton Publishing House, 1982)—for scholars; *Jesus and the New Age According to Luke* (St. Louis: Clayton Publishing House, 1972) and *Luke*, Proclamation Commentaries (Philadelphia: Fortress Press, 1976)—for general readers.]

51. See also Suetonius, *Augustus* 53.

52. Jesus is referred to as "Savior" (*sotēr*), for instance, in Luke 2:11 and Acts 13:23. The title "Leader" (*archēgos*) occurs in Acts 3:15; 5:31.

53. R. Morgenthaler, "Roma—Sedes Satanae," *Theologische Zeitschrift* 12 (1956): 289ff. I cannot go into detail here regarding Luke's highly consistent criticism of the "ruler ideology" of his time. It can only be described in the context of his entire Christology.

54. See W. Stegemann, "Lasset die Kinder zu mir kommen," in *Traditionen der Befreiung*, 1: 114–44. The "children's gospel" (Mark 10:13–16), too, must be read in this way, according to my interpretation.

55. Ibid., 117–25.

56. See L. Schottroff and W. Stegemann, *Jesus von Nazareth*, 16–24, 115.

57. Ibid., 113–19.

58. Von Harnack, *Mission and Expansion*, 1: 147.

59. In general, see von Harnack, *Mission and Expansion*, 1: 147–97. See also Gal. 6:10: "So then, as we have opportunity, let us do good to all men, and especially to those who are of the household of faith." Tertullian, who testifies especially to intra-Christian solidarity (*Apology* 39), is also aware of charity toward non-Christians: "our compassion spends more in the streets than yours does in the temples" (*Apology* 42; English translation in *The Ante-Nicene Fathers* [Grand Rapids: Wm. B. Eerdmans, 1951], III.49). Later, the Emperor Julian is compelled to grudgingly acknowledge the charity of the Christians (Sozomen, *Ecclesiastical History* V.16):

> For, while there are no persons in need among the Jews, and while even the impious Galileans provide, not only for those of their own party who are in want, but also for those who hold with us, it would indeed be disgraceful if we were to allow our own people to suffer from poverty. Teach the Pagans to co-operate in this work of benevolence, and let the first fruits of the towns be offered to the gods.

(English translation in *The Greek Ecclesiastical Historians* [London: Samuel Bagster and Sons, 1846], IV:233.) Especially in emergency situations of great proportions the Christians distinguish themselves by undiscriminating assistance (see Eusebius, *Ecclesiastical History* IX.8).

60. Eusebius, *Ecclesiastical History* IX.8.13–14:

> . . . while the proofs of the Christians' zeal and piety in every respect were manifest to all the heathen [during the black plague at the time of Maximin]. For example, they alone in such an evil state of affairs gave practical evidence of their sympathy and humanity: all day long some of them would diligently persevere in performing the last offices for the dying and burying them (for there were countless numbers, and no one to look after them); while others would gather together in a single assemblage the multitude of those who all throughout the city were wasted with the famine, and distribute bread to them all, so that their action was on all men's lips, and they glorified the God of the Christians, and, convinced by the deeds themselves, acknowledged that they alone were truly pious and God-fearing.

(English translation by J. E. L. Oulton. Vol. 2 of 2 vols. Loeb Classical Library [Cambridge: Harvard University Press; London: William Heinemann, 1932], 357.)

61. See in general H. Bolkenstein, *Wohltätigkeit*. For a concise overview see H. Bolkenstein and W. Schwer, entry on "Almosen,"

in *Reallexicon für Antike und Christentum* (1950), I: cols. 301–7; W. Schwer, entry on "Armenpflege," ibid., cols. 689–98; H. Bolkenstein and B. A. Kalsbach, ibid., entry on "Armut I," cols. 698–705. See also W.-D. Hauschild, "Armenfürsorge II," in *Theologische Realenzyklopädie* (1979), IV:14–23 (to be judged right critically in the case of the New Testament). As already mentioned, in the elder Seneca's *Controversies* (10:4), one of the motives for giving alms to begging children and youths is the grim possibility of their being one's own (abandoned) children or, conversely, the hope that others would give them alms as oneself does to these. The skeptical attitude toward almsgiving to beggars is evident in Diogenes Laertius (V.1, 17, 21).

62. This is further corroborated by the fact that Luke 11:41 and 12:32 are Lukan redactions. The "contents" of the vessels could hardly mean anything but food and drink.

63. Are those weeping widows wearing the garments themselves, or are they showing other garments remaining in the upper room, which had been made by Tabitha? It is commonly assumed that the widows were themselves the recipients of these alms (because they *were* widows). So they would have been wearing the garments; yet this seems rather like a "comic opera" scene to me: the women who received the alms gather around the deathbed of their benefactress and point to the alms on their bodies. As I see it, therefore, it is not by coincidence that Tabitha's body is laid out amid her alms; and, by the way, Peter throws out the widows quite unceremoniously *(ekbalōn)*.

64. For evidence supporting this view, see K. Berger, "Almosen für Israel," *New Testament Studies* 23 (1977): 180ff.

65. Ibid.

66. Ibid., 190–92.

67. See H. J. Degenhardt, *Lukas,* 160ff., 180ff. He does not distinguish adequately, however, between intra-Christian charity and solidarity with the poor. Conversely, his inquiry (into the difference) between "officers (of the church)" and other Christians is questionable.

68. S. Kierkegaard, "The Instant," in *Attack Upon Christendom* (Boston: Beacon Press, 1957), 181.

69. E. Käsemann, "Die endzeitliche Königsherrschaft Gottes," in *Kirchliche Konflikte* (Göttingen: Vandenhoeck & Ruprecht, 1982), 1:218.

70. See the interview with the head of the Protestant Church of

Germany delegation in Melbourne, Australia, in *Zeitschrift für ökumenische Begegnung und internationale Zusammenarbeit* 16 (1980): 32–33.

71. That he is a slave is evident from the parable itself: the rich man is his *kyrios* (Latin: *dominus*).

72. "To dig" (*skaptein*) has to be understood, I suspect, as a description of the miserable circumstances and toil of a farm slave or day laborer working on a farm. This is underscored by the simultaneous use of "to beg" (*epaitein*). Therefore, the steward must have had quite a comfortable position, even as a slave, if he fears these consequences.

73. Only then (Luke 16:9), after the parable is told, Jesus himself begins to speak. In v. 8 *kyrios* still refers to the rich slave owner, not Jesus. Note here the emphasis at the beginning of v. 9: "And *I* tell you, . . ."

74. The term *eklipē* (v. 9) hints at this: "so that when it *fails*." See also Luke 12:33: "with a *treasure* in the heavens *that does not fail*" (*thēsauron anekleipton*).

75. Luke uses a similar line of argument in 14:7–14. See also the analogous construction: objection by Pharisees (14:15 and 16:14).

76. This follows also from Luke 16:14–15, that is, the Pharisees are in fact lovers of money (*philargyroi*).

77. Among the voluminous literature on the "theology of the poor," I refer the reader to the following:

> *Bericht des Evangelischen Missionswerkes*, Evangelischer Pressedienst, Dokumentation No. 8/80: 35ff.
>
> Georges Casalis, "Das Evangelium der Armen," in *Traditionen der Befreiung* 1: 145–61 (English translation forthcoming from Fortress Press).
>
> Julio De Santa Ana, *Gute Nachricht für die Armen: Die Herausforderung der Armen in der Geschichte der Kirche* (Wuppertal, 1979).
>
> Norbert Greinacher, *Die Kirche der Armen: Zur Theologie der Befreiung* (Munich, 1980).
>
> José Míguez Bonino, *Doing Theology in a Revolutionary Situation* (Philadelphia: Fortress Press, 1975).
>
> [Also see Norman K. Gottwald, ed., *The Bible and Liberation: Political and Social Hermeneutics* (Maryknoll, N.Y.: Orbis Books, 1983), especially Part IV: Sociological Readings of the New Testament, 335–458.]

Index
of Passages

Biblical

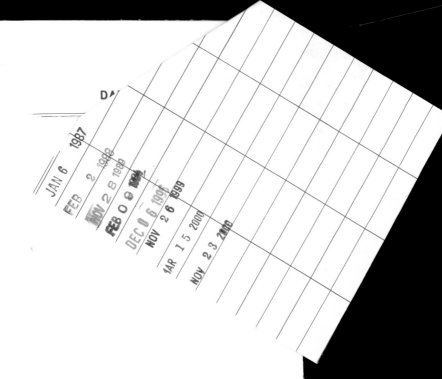